FLOWERS WE WILL NEVER KNOW THE NAMES OF

FLOWERS WE WILL NEVER KNOW THE NAMES OF

long poem

CATHY FORD

MotherTongue Publishing Limited
Salt Spring Island, BC
Canada

MOTHER TONGUE PUBLISHING LIMITED
290 Fulford-Ganges Road, Salt Spring Island, B.C. V8K 2K6   CANADA
www.mothertonguepublishing.com
Represented in North America by Heritage Group Distribution.

Copyright © Cathy Ford 2014. All Rights Reserved. The use of any part of this publication reproduced, transmitted in any form or by any means, electronic, mechanical, photocopying, recording or otherwise, or stored in a retrieval system, without the prior written consent of the publisher—or, in case of photocopying or other reprographic copying, a licence from Access Copyright, the Canadian Copyright Licensing Agency, info@accesscopyright.ca—is an infringement of the copyright law.

Book Design by Mark Hand
Front cover photograph by Janet Dwyer.
Typefaces used are ITC Giovanni and Monumenta.

Printed on Enviro Cream, 100% recycled
Printed and bound in Canada.

Mother Tongue Publishing gratefully acknowledges the assistance of the Province of British Columbia through the B.C. Arts Council and we acknowledge the support of the Canada Council for the Arts, which last year invested $157 million in writing and publishing throughout Canada.
Nous remercions de son soutien le Conseil des Arts du Canada, qui a investi 157$ millions de dollars l'an dernier dans les lettres et l'édition à travers le Canada.

LIBRARY AND ARCHIVES CANADA
CATALOGUING IN PUBLICATION

Ford, Cathy, author
    Flowers we will never know the names of : long poem / Cathy Ford.

ISBN 978-1-896949-48-2 (pbk.)

    1. Montréal École Polytechnique Women Students Massacre, Montréal, Québec, 1989--Poetry. I. Title.

PS8561.O64F56 2014   C811'.54   C2014-904849-1

for those with whom I first loved Montreal,
for December 6, 1989 and ever after,
for those who live there, in my heart, still
for women cherished, whether or not they ever know
for those of us gone too soon, lost innocents, dearly beloved,
and for all those suffering, lifelong, unspeakable loss

"Not being able to speak to thee with my lips, I write with flowers. I send thee this bouquet, a messenger from my soul. May its brilliant colors, its symmetry, and its perfume, be an emblem of her who loves thee."
—JEAN MARSH, "A Manner of Speaking," introduction to *The Illuminated Language of Flowers*

"Whether the flower or the color is the focus I do not know. I do know that the flower is painted large to convey to you my experience of the flower—and what is my experience of the flower— if it is not color."
—GEORGIA O'KEEFE, *One Hundred Flowers*

"I was painting in the quiet of my room, when I heard a rustling behind me. For a moment I thought someone was there, then I realised that the flowers I had left on a table were opening..."
—MARGARET MEE, *In Search of Flowers of the Amazon Forests*

"Siunakhoon ja jumal varjelkhoon"— "Bless us and save us all"
—translated from the Swedish

"A bouquet of flowers
so perfect you could never catch them all
such colours the heart ached.
Such colours, your heart ached."

"we are alone in the dark
whether we choose it or not

make no mistake about it

looking either older or younger than we are

          first blushes of winter

reading poetry in French, or some other language
we are not sure of
but cannot live without"

*"An unseen, perfect shroud
drooping from your shoulders along your back
a wing a long sweet wing,
dear, feathers falling from your body
like messages*
                              and other relationships between women
who care, continue to care."

IN MEMORIAM

Geneviève Bergeron, Hélène Colgan, Nathalie Croteau, Barbara Daigneault,
Anne-Marie Edward, Maud Haviernick, Barbara Klucznick Widajewicz,
Maryse Laganière, Maryse Leclair, Anne-Marie Lemay, Sonia Pelletier,
Michèle Richard, Annie St-Arneault, Annie Turcotte

CONTENTS

Flowers We Will Never Know The Names Of   1

Afterword   69

Notes on Text   75

Flowers We Will Never Know The Names Of

(for December 6th, 1989, and for Montreal)

I

Where there are flowers, white breath clouds hovering
over the heads of the emergency field, no one is moving fast enough
to bring back the dead

where there are flowers, wine red on the bodies of the fallen
their skin soft as petals of newly blooming *memento mori orchids*
in the hothouse of learning drifts winter snow

far away, hugging television screens to cold bellies for heat
this fertility of loathing, stark eyes of revelation, *evening stock, night stalks*
shining like horrified lanterns in the dark, trying not to birth itself
in the humidity of closed rooms, rooms no one can escape from, now or later

                       where there are sounds running the halls, winterborne

river of fear crossing one entire country
as if it were a railroad uniting the imagination, grieving snowblind
fearing the worst fearing the worst –

                Geneviève

Where there are flowers, butterfly of spring always flies out of metaphor, winter

butterfly soul of the dead, movement of heaven hurricanes interrogatives
galeforce from head to head in the richness of the border edging the path

wind here is winterchill, origami cutflower snowline textual
freezing the face into stark expressions of hopelessness, while we carry on, walking

stumbling the pathway, after the garden gate, I enter in,
the woman of the house greeting me before I step onto her porch
dizzy from the smell of tropical flowers gone wilde along her walk

what is that flower, I ask her, the name she does not know,
only that it blooms just once a year, only for one day, in northcoast wintertide
only a scent you cannot forget, just take it with you, as if blown into

    the bones of your skull, resonate

    imagination come alive, as if sleeping

only memory wakes us –

        Hélène

Flowers we will never know the name of
holy *death camus*, the white onion-skinned bulb, *citrine*
poison enough as it is sleeping under the earth, to kill

the *white snowflowers* of heaven, smell of sacred earth on your hands
how else does it go on, life and death of the flower, *snowdrop, snowfall*
leave just enough nothing is forgotten, so you are not forgotten, remembering

      delicacy, beautifulness, homeliness, comeliness, seduction

forgotten flowers the psyche of the living, alive this shock winterwhite blanket, as if
fabricate skin of calm acceptance, absolute mortality of all that is human
we are, after all, all only human - where does fear come from?

In this dichotomy of terror, there is no going on, keeping care
language-centred, write it down, what help for you is this

and yet, there are flowers, spring comes out of winter somehow
over and over – pure white morally or spiritually pure, it snows –

      Nathalie

4

Flowers we will never know
the names of

                    exhibitions of women explore the amazon of unknowing

by water-borne imagining, by hardship, by canoe, by climbing mountains of reality,
broken in spirit, or *unbroken*, broke back

making up this northern tropical zone, conservatory plantarium
we are never as attentive, as sensitive, as perceptive
as our hopes, *desire thereby to create something freely, find something new*

fallow ground, and yet, go on, breaking raw trails on top of old ones rediscovered
entering into wilderness never lost, not even in wintertime, its snowy parable
refound strange exotic erotic blooms whose names some woman has already uttered

if only we could have heard her then, change abrupt as blizzard or chinook
thought of her voice as an aria, *solo voice with instrumental accompaniment*

                  rhapsody, a warning – ice thawn, crystalline

                  Barbara

In flowers, a language where one word, a naming, is breath,
is voice, is soul
language as foreign as stars, as separate as planets

mechanics of perception, the intellect, engineered like complicity
winterbourne, stream that flows only in winter, spirit river

        there are women who wander into changing the world

no one knows their name when first they meet them on the road

as easily, as eager a constellation of biology
as students innocent of translation
as free of chemistry as a miracle, a single snowflake
before it is taken apart, microscoped, melting

        as preface free of premonition as tragedy –

we will lose you and never find you again, eye, heart, *oriflamme*
or soul's telescope to the heavens –

        Anne-Marie

A language, flowered, *means* breath, *means* voice, *means* soul give me

precision optics of the heart

the open and close of the truth
so I can sleep at night, thinking
how it keeps me alive, summer, winter, oratorio frantically

accuses me of concentration on the icy macabre

yet it does not matter, this death-dealing, this insomniac mania
which bullets enter which part of the body – *I understand nothing* – whiteout

only this relief, doesn't matter anymore when you are gone

but once the brain was thought not to function at all
but to shelter, to covenant, protect the heart, and lungs, to cool, temper

it makes no sense, it never will

yours is the voice gone, your particular way of speaking, your thinking –

Maud

A bouquet of flowers,

         thrown on the tracks, your tracks in snow

in a country where all the trains do not run any more, or on time

eventually, one or two dry ice petals frozen
to the wheels of the transcanada, transcontinental, transmountainous

         reach across miles of uncertainty, disbelief

the things we are sure of,

         to do with bodies, colour, naming, winterkill

heritages and histories, recitatives, text messaging

         but politics, violence, again and again

confuses, makes us act as if we know everything
(knowing nothing)
as if we are sure
(dying of uncertainty) –

         Barbara

Flowers, in bouquet, arrived in the hand

                        and falling apart, petals adrift earthbound like snow

I am carrying now, and forever
a simple, single flower as my bouquet to you, *as if I was a virgin bride*

in this nightmare I know nothing, only that master death is on the stairs

inadequate as a child at the threshold of life, uncomprehending
but willing to walk slowly, at first cautious as the arrival of a gentle winter
into this auto-da-fe, the never-ending questions, unending, *why*, and
how will your dying be dealt with,

will anyone note your passing, once it is old news,
once the obscenity screen, the bad news papers have gone cold

once lost, those who actually, laying on of their hands, touched your life
with fire, with faint,

              grasp of who you really are –

        Maryse

So many flowers, the mind is dazed with revolution
delirious with effort and desire for change, uncensored

schools every action, even the post-humous granting of degrees, in snow

the budgeting of every moment of love –
what return is there for commitment, now you've been selected out

                how peaceful the grey glove lies on the pianoforte

we will never know whose glove this is

waiting for her hand to come
who carried the flowers, who played the symphony, over and over again
of the sister of Mozart, over-practicing in the winterdark, manic with perfection

as if she was the one who had composed everything unexpected
she knew it all by heart, icicles snapped off the end of a line –

as if the tonal transitions that made sense
only make sense to her, if played by her own hand –

            Maryse

10

The revolution, dazed with flowers and blinding snow
halts and pushes and halts its cart in the street
bleeding bits of colour over the cobblestones - pushes on again

there is no stopping the inexorable, *en français*, winterkilling

                        no, we shall not cease to witness –

when I was a little girl, fireborne, only pale air and frozen water, I knew
pallid as skating winterborne, the river frozen wild and freedom long
every day crack lined with possibility

                        never having met you, sanctuary earth,

we would meet one day, though yours is not yet my first language

this is how flowers grow, all in a row, in chaos, in rapture, simplicity, in peace

when the war is over, spaces between filled for the ones no longer there, pretty maids
all the places not yet been to – as for me, I have never been to Paris, France –

not even in winter - and suffer this, only a little like silence –

                        Anne-Marie

Unnamed, unknown, flowers without artifice
fight against autocratic content, dead form, battle of the elite for art
untouched by reality, tyranny

how does one go on

the journalistic avoidance of the truth, such power trembles

the ghosts of gardens

out the window

even in winter, always in summer, covered in snow

pale outline of the hibernating possibility of being alive, it looks as if

you are sleeping, there, warm and awake, wintry interpretations of dreams as life

somewhere under the snow
there are flowers, the wildness in them
beating like a tiny heart in each one, an ovary, full of all the eggs you will ever
release, one by one, all that maturing into a void –

Sonia

12

Flowers, unknown, unnamed, *fall on my knees*, nameless
dread full of the kind of pretension, and deadline a day
series of moments like this one, sheds onto the winter garden

angel in the snow appearing, gazes down
arms folded around her chrysalis body like wings, just like caught wings –
bouquet of flowers in her hand — the last leaf on the flowering plum tree

dried dormant the colour of old blood, like a hummingbird poised to drink
its nectar-filled life out of winter, the winterwood of a spring-blooming tree,
dry snap branch that will leaf again, *promises, promises*

this breath of life should have tried already to wend its way south, its pursuit, guise, gaze
its imaginary fruit flowering the purple of placenta, the bulging unseamed shape

pregnant the pauses fall like petals down, the maple leaves

will you come again up to the window – *will I once more see you - understand*

you were everything to me –shadow's shape moving winter into small, perfect, woman –

Michèle

The flowers that cannot be named, language

                    we feel but cannot say

words gather icicle sharp in our throats, we cannot cry out

the names of our mothers who suffered like this
our own names, out of fear, out of pain, our sisters, daughters

out of the untold stories of histories of women, grandmothers, granddaughters

words strangle up out of the earth, like the first *tulip* shards in December,
translucent shy tenderness of *snow drops*, the very idea of *violets*, in snow

the colours our bodies drift to, lutescent, the front window winter display
an urban flower shop, blooms out into the street like a glasswalled garden
on the way to class, we drop our books, our ideas, library, and *lean like heaven*

                    into the peace of flowers, fresh flowers, flowers in winter

knowing we have so far, made nothing greater than this –

still is the dream, it *is* possible –

            Annie, and again, *Annie*

14

To express what cannot be said in words,
the language of flowers – **a**pple blossom, temptation, **a**pricot *muteflower*

scatter once these over your memory and hold fast the caring...

because, **a**buse not, said in your name: *crocus, red* **a**maryllis, **a**lmond *for hope*
because you have, **a**ffection beyond the grave: *green locust tree*

alas for my poor heart, I miss you: *deep red carnation*, January, forgiving, *dark iris*

because, **a**nguish colours my days: *the June red rose, I love you*
because, I am among the **a**shamed: *Japan roses, winter* **a**conite

because of your **b**eauty, unconscious: *the **b**urgundy rose, death's head lily*
because you were **b**etrayed: *white catchfly, snowball,* sterile white flowers, schooled
beware: *oleander, aster,* an afterthought, September, October, November
blackness will fall you all down: *ebony tree, artemsia, blown poppies,* delicate as

breasts: *the cream tulip* cupped in your ethereal hands, December
breath: *lily-throated thrush, azalea,* temperance, this evocation of spirit
bury you amid nature's beauties: *persimmon, nicotiana, twice bloomed,*
                    those of us who love you

the price of forgetting, **c**alumny: *hellebore, madder*
colour of my fate: *coral honeysuckle, the red canna, ochre primrose*

there is no **c**onsolation, solace: *red poppy, meline tearose*
but **c**onstancy: *giant pyramidal bellflower, amber aurulent*
and **c**ourage: *black poplar, bachelor's buttons,* the sadness of **c**elibacy, deathwatch

cremation posie, fleur, lush masses, crush of flowers, visual brilliance, *everlasting*
what **c**rime was done you: *tamarisk,* the only joy left eloquence

daphne flower papier woven stronger than linen, truth is stronger than…

sweet **d**aphne maidenhead, your flowering pressed makes paper
that interwoven fabric of my life

the study of being alive, death, beauty
those seeking the beautiful must find it, somehow, somewhere, least expected

what **d**anger walked into your life: *rosebay rhododendron, white trumpet flower,*
                      harbinger of **d**eath, **d**anger, and fear

death, walking: *cypress, snow-on-the-mountains,* quiet as a blanket of snow
deceit: *dogsbane, sicksweet basil,* hatred then, death comes down
deception: *the winter white cherry tree, canary vitelline,* cold, quiet

ah, here is my **d**eclaration of love: *a red tulip solitary,* prostration before love
keep me from **d**espair: *marigold, whiteflower* cups inflorescences

save me from **d**espondency: *humble plant, luteous*
rather, **d**evotion: *peruvian heliotrope*

dedication, billet **d**eux bouquets, the creative art of writing abecedary

bluebell: constancy, sorrowful regret and yet gratitude
blue hyacinth: another constant heart

    your sister for whom it will be now
    as if she never had a sister

except you, your age stopt

yellow broom: your humility and faith everlasting, glossology

dead, the beloved, *butterfly flower*, soul of the **d**ying

    your sisters all left alone

striped carnation: refusing to forget, **d**ownwind caught *calendula*, next October

when first explorers by sea saw B.C., entered jungle they expected, *glory*

begild yellow carnation: love undiminished, **d**espite **d**isdain, hardening off

my very first speaking, *bird, pretty bird*, from the garden, *fool narcissus*
uncompromising sense of achievement, free-form only one's own path, wandering

wintergreen, evergreen: ringing white bell-shaped flowers, funerary chamber of the heart
white carnation: next November

yellow mum: slighted, hopeless love rescued, *aurulence, articulata*

red chrysanthemum: I still love you, *white chrysanthemum*, truth

we may speak no longer in the tongues we have memorized
but must begin again with life, being alive, *pearl-drops-in-snow*
overwinter communicating by unmurdered means
as if there was still hope, scattered like *wedding rose* petal wishes

    *your father cannot believe you are **dead***

love without end: ***d****affodil*, your brother your one lost sweet brother

d*ahlia:* instability and reckless splendor combined, ***d****aisy,* your valiant innocence

white rose: radiated, transmitted, reflected light, containing
all the colours of the visible spectrum, *what **d**oes it cost*

your husband your lover there is no other

d*ianthus: mort violente,* make haste mercy, *engilt winterlily*

    *the sorrow of your **d**ying is so **d**eep*
    *like **d**eath your **d**ying does not stop*

rather, **d**ignity: *laurel-leaved magnolia,* love of nature

give me **d**ignity of mind: *hundred-leaves rose,* white for worthiness
do you justice: *chestnut, in flower*
done you wrong: *billy holiday, gardenia*

in my **d**reams: *osmunda tree,* your mother who brought you up by herself
dying to see you, and where are you now: *virginia creeper* of my bookshelves
sweet mauve burdock, french marigold, jealousy, *false oriental poppy*

looking for **e**nergy in adversity: *chamomile, venus flytrap*
recover these **e**xtinguished hopes: *major convolvulus, flowering sage,* lifeforce grace

cut down in your prime, before your time
force fainting the vibrantly alive, **d**affodil, and again, **d**affodil **n**arcissus, in snow

you were the **f**ai̠rest of the young: *pearl drops,* in the coldest season of the year
for **f**aithfulness: *blue violet,* **F**ebruary, as if sprung from obscurity, *winterberry*

in **f**arewell: *michaelmas daisy, garden anemone,* **f**orsaken
fate, the dark side: *hemp-wound* your hair, *fuschia,* grace of a girl

flower of sweet marsh, licked tears, frozen

flame of the ones who love you: *fleur-de-lis, red poppy No. VI, red canna 1924*
forget you not: *forget-me-not, mouse-eared scorpion grass*

that you were **f**ree-flowering: *aspasia lunata, the brazilian orchid*
fresh wounds bleeding into the December snow: *red roses*

neither *red **g**eranium* for comfort, nor ***g**ladiolus* in August
this bower of flowers across a nation

no secluded grove of trees and flowers
no covering just one casket or grave, robbing sunlight, air

this **g**rief will never leave me: *aloe, harebell, seagreen anemone,* griefstricken

laburnum: **h**ail forsaken, winterer, *ornamental deadly nightshade,*
atropine

have pity on my passion, **h**earty *jonquil* in March, **h**eather for solitude
the **h**eartlessness of your murderer I will not forget: *hydrangea*
the **h**opeless, not **h**eartless fight for your remembering: *love lies bleeding*

hawthorne, tone my heart now, steady its beat, strengthen the measure
too much is poison, too little, ah well

give me **h**ope in adversity: *spruce pine*, your sweet scented body

keeping always the **h**orror of your dying in front of me: *creeping cereus,*
mandrake, dragonswort, snakesfoot

I attach myself to you: *Indian jasmine,* kindness, *black petunia, white morning glory with dark heart*

I change but in death: *bay leaf, black iris*
I declare against him, the one who shot you dead: *belvedere, wild licorice*

I die if neglected, you have died: *laurestina, red canna 1923*
your grandmother when
I have lost all faith in your freedom to be freely alive: *mourning bride*

brides of christ: married for peace of mind, heartfull
poet maudite: **I** live for you
passionflower of the apocalypse: the nunnery garden

virginals: fecundity of the herb and flower beds, it's winter

women as healers, common as the *common buttercup*
begonia: begone these worried hearts, winterly
trailing lobelia: where are you sleeping, community of women

love lies weeping: in darkness is loneliness, *wintersnow* flowering

wise woman, *inkberry, black alder*, persist over winter
laying on of hands, the white garden, all snowy white, wintering

simply, **I** live for thee: *cedar leaf*, between winter solstice, vernal equinox

I shall die tomorrow: *gum cistus, ivy* for friendship alone
think only of your **i**mmortality: *amaranth globe, petunia and coleus 1924*

your grandmother then

knowing you, **i**ncorruptible: *cedar of lebanon, sacred tree,*
beloved mistress of my **i**mpolitic heart

above all, take your **i**nnocence with you: *white rose*, soul of the *white rose*

above all, **j**ustice: *rudbeckia, chestnut tree,* full pink-centered white snow
flower cascading, *white camellia,* excellence

justice shall be done: *coltsfoot, calla lilies* advancing to take back night
in your dreams, *amaryllis belladonna*

justice shall be done in your name: *sweet-scented tussilage, purple petunia
No. 2, 1924,* after all

*j*onquil, have pity on my passion, spent, so spent

keep me inside your heart, I always love you: *poinsettia, red, white,*
                hedges from my deepest dreams, interiority,
                green smell of leaves, immigrant shiny in Caribbean rain
                Bequia, 1986, hedges taller than fairy tales,

        honey writing billet-doux
        what will save us
                maiden blush, declarations, hedges
                      overheight

blueish breathless flowers: rhetorical as winter snow, *Swedish **kalmia***

lady's slipper waiting your rest: *paphiopedilum stonei (clitoris) orchid*

longing, female flower: *honeysuckle*, generous affection, *jasmine*, kindness

*l*arkspur: unfaithfulness redeemed, by July
all mistrust salvaged: *lavender*, you are

*l*ilac: like first love, effortlessly, *snowflake amàryllis*, without regret
or *lily of the valley*: end of May, luck and good fortune returned

flower of the month, petals a snowfield of narrative truth, relief to the soul
in many babels, amidst confusion of tongues, voices, languages, sounds,

      up the tower's stair, *luminato*
on every tumultuous step, a bouquet

soul's deep sorrow, languishment

lorraine, alsace, flowers on rock, flowers in snow
lush in language in which the sacred, religion, the word
means book, high mountain flowered cave text is holy
petals blown dust in cliff chapters, charcoal drawn, sacrificed crypt flowers
to leave this message, love, beloved

using words dangerous with sentiment, intention
lest you not be forsaken

to freely speak, loving
words of friendship, the connection of sympathy and passion, compassion

the language of flowers, this delicate beauty overwintered, impending
experience our only colour wheel, torture catharining an art form

lamentation never ceasing: *aspen tree* in every memorial park, by
every flowing river, whitewater

"like love its deep heart is full", the country will not forget

you: *sensitive plant,* every touch a memory

life, you never had enough: *lucern, cup of silver, icicleflower*

malevolence, struck you down: *lobelia*
your **m**artyrdom: a bouquet of fourteen *red roses*
melancholy: *the dark geranium of recall*
memory: *syringa, the light iris,* opening out to dawn, purpose and intent

after all this, what will I do, what **m**essage: *blind iris, snowbells*

midnight tears dry on my face: ***m**iltonia echo bay orchid*
mourning, forever and for ever after: *weeping willow*

she leans into

                life's **m**illstream, *black narcissus,* life going on,

like **m**int: for wisdom, *opheliaflower,* **m**yrtle, love enduring

my regrets follow you to the grave: *asphodel, ashflower,* I cannot forget
the first words I heard of your dying

never-ceasing remembrance: *ever-lasting, the dark iris, lesbia*

night falls: *blue convolvulus,* **n**ight *convolvulus,* bleeds white
not to forget: *rosemary,* modesty, **n**ight *jasmine,* kind hearted in sorrow

"**n**othing compares to you": *portulacca, four o'clocks, martyrfleur*

orchidaceae: *cattleya violacea*, innocence and purity, *deaf jasmine*, dead

painting the lily: *daphne odora*, gilded saints and holy women
perseverance: *canary grass, ground laurel, european sweet-briar, swamp magnolia, snowberry*, **p**ink flower, white berry

untainted the work women will do in your names, *the little birds, the deltas of venus*, **p**rick of conscience, smell of *vagina magnolia* before the death-dealing lay down their weapons, **p**ity epistolary, sighs

***p**inks:* uttering deathly sweet as well as silence may

pity these kinds of murderers do not know what is coming, **p**itiful: *pine*

precaution (***p**recautions against death*) the work done in your names:
golden rod, tall hollies, evergreen blooming

poetry: *eglantine*, I wound to heal

flowers against evil, breviary

prayer for your recovery, your very existence, *orchidaceous*, unfound,
unrecorded, unpainted, undone

the name of a flower which rhymed with its name, your name spelling

prediction: in my lifetime, this killing must stop, ***p**rophetic marigold*

queen of the night: blooms once yearly, one nightfall, its perfume heady,
aromatic, it closes its eye at sunrise, *black tulip*

queen of everything, any hour, day or night, I will know you, intimacy, *in
to me I see: iris*, your eyes, deep purpled cornea,
flesh, your naked interiors, how I love you, your

regard: in your names, I have planted *one hundred daffodils* in snow

regret: *r*ue, nothing will ever be enough, *yellow rose* for jealousy, envy

remember: *cattleya memoria, the orchid, cream narcissus*, in consideration

remembrance: *pheasant's eye*, deep thoughts, *pansy*, eye of sorrow ·
        looking up, *which flowers are these…*

resistance to loss of you, prime of your short, sweet lives: *tremella nestoc*

resolved to win, war against the bodies of women: *purple columbine,*
                purple and black suffrage colours, remember…

Turkish, Arabique, Brazilian, French, Holland bulbs, I love you, glossia,

rose, may you be pleased, *eloquence,* I love you,
may all your sorrows be mine
this multilingual cryptology, mothertongue, free with affection

covetous only of time, little books of the language of flowers

conflicted seldom by ambition, pasigraphy legalese, nightletters

resolute with love: *whitewood, tulip tree, linden, cottonwood flower*
                              drifted snow, *lingua franca, argot*

responsive, now and forever, to the opened look in your eye

revenge, not a word many women use, *writing well is the best* **r**evenge,
                              she
said, **r**evenge: *birdsfoot, trefoil, snowplant,* hanging **r**ed berries, no leaves

sadness: *dead leaves*, what has been left of you, on iced ground
secrets: the kind women will not keep any more, *yellow acacia*

shame: in your name, men will hang their heads in **s**hame, **s**orrow

asking for forgiveness, the penance of deserving,
                               desire, the reckoning before they touch

the body
of any woman, even in love, **s**hame, *whitely peony*, *snowlimit blossom*

sickness: *zephyr flower*, the only name or excuse for your dying

silence: *belladonna*, of the **s**oul, women will not be **s**ilent now

sleep: *the white poppy*, unto death, of the way you will be remembered,
                                even

in the **s**leeping of the women who **s**peak love in
your names

soul language **s**peaking: *psyche flower*
spirit: *purple hyacinth*, pain unremitting

p q r s again again
even the alphabet stumbling, quiet, this death quiet scrutiny of sanity,
insanity

how to employ, make use, creation and utilization, *crazy buds, field daisy*
what budding this, which flower acres and acres of *white overnight poppies*
the white garden
from the French, this flower language

untranslatable

satin flower: honesty, it is a virtue, isn't it, *nightshade,*
campanulate, bell-shaped, ringing down tears
scotch thistle: retaliation, neither to die or to kill by winter cold
you are the ones who cannot be, who can never be, mourned enough

mourner's bride, snapdragon: refusal to accept the hatred of men
even if practiced politely on the bodies of women, or their minds
glimmered as water, as dew dropped on the gatekeeper's path

snowdrop: solace and hope, in the snow, ironic
sunflower: arrogance forgotten, *night-blooming cereus*
sweetpea: April, devastated by loss, never quite recovered
yet determined to live, whatever season

sweet william: gallantry then, nakedness of language, its politik

strawflower: suffer me to be your slave, willing handmaiden

healer to legacy of pain, taught to prefer whitework embroidery of winter
stitching petals like tears to the quilt bedding

quieting the shivering fearsome dark

rosebud: first love, young love, youthfulness, I love you utterly
rose red: may you be pleased with my love and all your sorrows be mine

*princessflowe*r: from this you will know me, guileless *chastetree*

in the garden I grew up in, gold and silver, bronze dusted flowers tall,

spun fairytales, *climbing roses,* made a cave to nestle in
winter palace offerings fit for an empress, *josephine, winter budding*

tiny nightraven birds chittered quiet as *lover's mist,* rustled my waiting ear

garnet stocks embroidered grande platinum metallic as a queen's sceptre
purple royal and midnight medieval blue, nighttide artless
inexpressive as *white moon in black cloud*, photo negative of history

lilac and *blush lilac, blush lily,* and *paperwhite,* I was born there
as dizzy with bees as honey, *immaculata* happiness protection from

the other world of the flower bouquet, netherworld

because you died I send flowers

a language much lost in transcription

sorcery, witchcraft: *enchanter's nightshade,* eaten at peril of death, the last
rationale for the killing of women
by the self-appointed, the last metaphor women
have undone, still work to undo, six million
women falsely accused, millions more women
uncounted, unknown, undead, it goes on, with
fourteen more, dead, dying, of

sorrow: *yew, oriental poppies,* if only taking *red opium poppy* would help
with forgetting, instead it imprints the soul,
makes the features of the countenance grow old
before our eyes, how can anyone make this
poetry, the work that must over and over
and over again, be done, polite correspondence
irretrievably lost, bloodred morphology

the grief, endless, *the washing of bodies*

spell in winter: *circaea*, never-forgetting anesthesia of the conscious,
colour of women who cherish one another, numbed
to threat of difference, is there any diffidence **s**o
terrible, so like *medusaflower* **s**he freezes the soul…

spell: write down your names in the book of remembering, yours
and all the others, just as different as me, *tiger lily, black-eyed **s**usan*

suffering: *thistle*, unique wild field flower that cannot be killed

sympathy: *balm, thrift*, waste not, winterize, winterfeed

tears: *helenium*, what names you are remembered by, rain that fell
icicles the night your deaths made the national

news, rain on this side of the country, while
you died in snow, in wind, cold darkened rooms
*yellow Karsh **t**ulip*, this impossible love, so rare

the survivors from a madman's hit list, cut sliced down
to say **t**hank you to the living is not enough

this heart's mystery: *crimson polyanthus*, I am not the only one so affected
by losing you, wild and winter flowers, I will
never know the names of, as if I have known
you

forever, thoughts of absent friends: *zinnia*, brings you to mind, times I
visited Montreal, spent days there crawling on
my hands and knees in the front garden planting
and replanting the perennials, mixed annuals for
balance, for change, *rose of sharon*, I
miss you, your coral, peach, orange, luminous in
the night, like the colour photograph of a naked
woman's body engraved on the eye

the fact is, sans sympathy, I miscarried my last child in your
lost love, trace lily
garden, *plancenta plant*, *placentae*, four, *previa*, ones never known

thistleflower: fidelity, *milkweed*, we are blown like whitened flowerheads
torn pinwheels into the wind, female shapes underneath a blanket of snow

tomorrow I shall die: *cistus,* but not like you, is there such hope still
          growing in the garden of my mind, even while
          I know too much, remember too many statistics,
          revision too many nightmares, is there any hot-
          house departure from this horror, this shocking
          realization, this self-indulgence I cannot shed as
          if it was an old winter coat, or the outside leaves
          of the slow-flowering fear that I too am not safe,
          the slow-flowering

touch-me-not: *burdock, red balsam, fringed polygala,*
treachery: *bilberry,* I know your names, *lavender-flowered wintergreen*
treason: *whortleberry,* I hear your names in the night, sacrifice

truth: you are *bittersweet nightshade, narcisscis,* the last *rainforest orchid,*
          you must be spoken

self-interest given over, December, tenderest brilliants lifting out of snow

unceasing remembrance: *cudweed, black hollyhock, blue larkspur*

unexpected meeting: *lemon geranium*, my face in the mirror every morning, how like every woman I am, just a woman, is there any reason at all for this

unfading love: *amaranth globe*, even in winter, I know you by heart

vagina: if all else fails, I know you, *virginflower, catasetum orchid, jack-in-the-pulpit,*
                    you can't fool me, I will not neglect what I know

                    virgin's bower: female spiritual beauty

war against the bodies of women, I know too much,
achillea millefolia, milfoil, york and lancaster rose, mounds and mounds
and grave-mounds of roses,

never forgetting, *sweet violet* -
from obscurity blossoming, spell of power
unseen sustenance, unsupported luminosity
- keeps and releases its perfume even after death

veronica: fidelity, *yellow violet*, rural happiness, *sweet modesty*, it snows
varily: remove my heart from the crush of the city, any city, *dropped posy*
violet everlasting: purple spelling *suffrage*, power intact despite everything

warning: *hand-flower tree (the **w**ork of our hands)*, **w**omen will prevent
the **w**ar against **w**omen, **w**omen will reveal

watchfulness: if you haven't heard me, you haven't been listening, *dame
violet* bloomed against **w**hite ground

winter: *the guelder rose, roses in snow*, for you, meritorious
worthiness beyond beauty: *calla lily, sweet alyssum*, cause no harm, above
all, do no harm, you are, **w**orth beyond beauty

worthy of all praise: *fennel*, these fourteen can never be replaced, remade,
redone, rewritten, revisioned, please remember
in total darkness, only our own fears protect us,
flatter our strengths. In frozen ground, only other
bodies protect us, shelter us **w**anting, and **w**arm us
through, and through, flowers **w**ildly cultivated

ribbon my soul with flowers not yet seen, named, hothouse jungle
greenhousing enculturated

yet in winter, the *stillbirth waterlilies* still blooming, floatfaced under ice
those *winterlilies*, funereal scent of hallucination, near death, induced
coma
waiting, turn upon return

wallflower: felicity in adversity, affection, alive, an existing flower
language

***w**aterlily*, and again, ***w**hite **w**inter **w**aterlilies*
*the **w**hite peace lily* emboldens
how sorrowful the hearts of those who love you
think of your dying, desperate for peace

in the space between breaths you are gone
the space between flowers, transformed

                        in acceptance only that the dead never leave

***w**ild hyacinth*: the heart's constancy, memory, idyll
despite unnatural acts or fearfulness, exposure to excessive cold, snow, ice

***w**ild lily, **w**ilde orchidlily*: fawn-coloured, struggle for calm acceptance
of absolute mortality, how to reconcile

remembering and forgetting
like a life created like a work of art, frozen in time, captured

***w**indflower*: blessed by forgetfulness, **w**orthy, **w**orthwhile

that kind of winter that is about cold, fear
madness, violence against women

freezing the heart

*x*anthium: rudeness, pertinacity, refrain of defensiveness,
self-absorbed protection of oneself and others, hermit-like,
in the handmirror

finding oneself still alive, fired to make change, affect
botanicals, anatomicals

young women looking old, as if they have already died alone
and fearful, for whom there is no redemption and life everlasting

the anniversary bouquet, the seasons wood, steel, lace, agate, ivory, glass
china, silver, the years go by, frost freeze, scrapeglaze like windows

polish clear the silver tea set, all faces, memories caught in burning snow

don't forget, do not be forgotten, what if **y**ou cannot forget

"because they were women"

x-ray of my heart's pulse, colour-dyed from the soul's passion, articulate
as
                           colour of the flesh, the opened eye, *sweet almond,*
                           absinthe flower, sweet forgetting, mellifluence,
nectareous

you are cold: *hortensia*, cold in the ground, my loved one, and I am
                             awake now to **y**ou never being here again, and I
                             cannot go back to sleep, not now

you are my divinity: holy ones, *cowslip*, humility **y**our middle name, name
                         in the dark, expressive as the word for winter

you are the perfection of female loveliness: *justicia, delicate flower*

you will be my death: *hemlock*, work unceasingly to put a stop to violence
                      against women and children, trust me on this
                      epistolary sighs, passionate declarations

 your charms are engraven on my heart: *spindle tree, giant white peony,*
                  you inspire, I cannot, choose not, to forget **y**ou

your language as if flowers, notwithstanding, flowers as another language,
your literature, scented love letters cannot avoid politics, personal position

your looks freeze me: *ice plant*, the body of **y**our body covered with a
                    white sheet, carried through snow

your presence softens my pains: always **y**ou are with me, I know what
                        signifies, *milkvetch, common weeds families* I
                        cannot live without, breath of my beloved I
                        cannot disavow, *white rose No. 3, ballet skirt*, or
                        electric light 1927, how I love **y**ou

anyone who thinks now I have fallen
in love utterly with death itself, how mistaken, how I keep on searching

chastising the word horror for its inadequacy
murder for its lack of precision, bullets sprayed

sorrow for its leaving you behind, breathless, on the stairs
unable to get up again, stand, at the minute

your purity equals **y**our loveliness: *orange blossom*, I will travel the river
                        lethe to visit **y**our happiness again, cross over

your qualities are unequaled: *peach blush,* **y**our fragility a shock to the
                        soul, spirit of living quivers at **y**our wintersnow
                        fragrance, *sweet hearted water lily,* floats on the
                        river of death, do **y**ou see her too in **y**our mind's
                        eye, the *empress lotus* meditates, perfumed like
                        heaven, *white geisha lilies,* dying, purity of
                        heart

your qualities surpass **y**our charms: *mignonette,* what name shall I call **y**ou
                        but dear ones, darlings

your sorrows mine: *obsidian rose, queen of the night black tulip*

beyond alphabet

your names on my lips forever: *melancholia, holy flower*, if you think I am
       sentimental you haven't heard me yet, not yet,
       anger, rage and retribution, I am planting flowers, armfuls of
       flowers, all that is valued
       useful, such truth and beauty, sound of the
       water, ocean, peace. Smell of salt. Sand. Grit.
       Wet logs. In geography so far away from you,
       reach for comprehension will not leave me.

Red edible berries clung to the branches through all your winters.

Your river reaches for the sea, brimming sea of life, *the sea is also a*
       garden, saffron lily, all falsehood revealed,
       paperwhites on the desktop
       elegiacally transformative, all is perhaps not
       vanity

after all

youthful, gladness, innocence, love: has all this been said, *spring crocus,*
ash flower, white lilac, red catchfly, **y**our lives
gone free, I cannot forget, 14 funeral boats, 14

candles, 14 *red fleur-de-lis,* 14 *red carnations,*
14 *gilded straw wheat stalks,* 14 *maple leaves*

paper more paper
lantern boats float out like greenhouse flowers
reblooming into the red tideline, lit *aureate*

yet, late arriving, a nascent child wanders into the ceremony
crying as if everything is lost, as if there cannot ever be tears sufficient

eyes quadrafoliats, wide open flower symbols sculpted in old soul gold
buried in ancestral ceremony, sarcophagus lining, red velvet ground

bejeweled, fashionista, winterista, dressed in black
those of us westdressed pitchblack, even funereal, stand out snowshadows

yellows lily: survival struggle, remembrance, *cremation zinnia*, white bone
yielding: in snow, the death of fourteen Montreal women, my beloveds

zealousness: *elderberry, miracle flower, peace lily,* how can I come to you being gone, what bouquet this, to place at your feet, over your sweet memory, where are you now, what sorrow this, your dying example, fragile hope, if all else fails, if I and all those alike, fail, if there are yet lost, undiscovered, undisclosed, other flowers we will never know the names of, bouquets inadequate to the dedication, women, fine women, at least, dare, just burn this, woefully insignificant…Ashes to ashes. Poem. Do not forget. And yet. Be responsible. Abuse not. *I have nothing to say.* Murder not. *I cannot speak of this.* Never. *I will not be silenced.* December 6. Some are flowers. Roses. Remembrance. By any other unknown name. Do not. Forgetting. Burn this poem.

AFTERWORD

I N MY SMALL ISLAND COMMUNITY, November 21, 1994, at a planning event preceding our now annual commemoration of December 6, 1989, Frances Wasserlein spoke to the women of WAVAW, Women Against Violence Against Women. Speaking on the issue of the experience of violence against women, she said, "Now is the time to refuse to be among the silenced. To say, I am a feminist. To stand up in order to prevent the silence once again to fall."

The silence of intense sympathy, grief and loss had indeed fallen that winter day, across Canada. When the violence of the morning of December 6, 1989 stopped, it was at first, very quiet. Many grief-stricken women who still had a voice were slow to speak up, but they did. Women now changed forever, moved their grief to action, out of nightmare, to healing, to artistic expression, to commemorative events, and although these women moved with determination, many were still raw with pain after what had occurred at L'École Polytechnique. Their work was inseparable from the cold facts, the mournfulness across Canada, yet activism persisted.

I needed a voice for the material I had in mind, in draft, to avoid falling not into silence, this I already refused, but into some kind of abyss, where I could not speak my sorrow, my rage, my passion, my overt feminist politics and poetics, with clarity or peace of mind, or without speaking violence back. Following accident and inclination, through the first years after the Montreal Massacre, while continuing to work on the issue of violence against women in my own community, I found the language of flowers, a female tradition, practiced all around me by women whose gardens, watercolours, oil paintings, novels, embroidery, quilting, I loved, all flower-celebrating arts perfected by the Victorians, and still cherished.

Historically, I've often been drawn to stories of Turkish and Arabian women, some of these women covered, secluded, isolated emotionally, physically, politically or culturally, who sent letters to one another using flowers, and their meanings, in message bouquets. Messages of artistry, support, love, celebration, sorrow, warning. Flowers attached to verse interpretations in poetry. Other women reached beyond their daily lives into creative artistic work, in sending flowers, in growing gardens, in becoming painters, writers, artists of all kinds. With hope and love and healing, despite all the odds, women through the centuries had continued to express themselves with language arts related to beauty, even out of their experiences of repression, domestic violence, terrorism, the horrors of war and the perpetration of female genocide upon themselves, their lives, other women.

The whole colour wash of the writing that interested me moved into darker places, as if the full life force of the young women who had died in Montreal had moved to a kind of darkness on the colour wheel, entry wounds graven into language and the longing for rebirth and renewal after such pain. The long poem I was working on set itself down more than once through those years, resting only to grow again, examining silence, attempting to push boundaries of vocabulary and image, to allow the poetry to find its own form and content, new to its author.

I was writing out of that place of sorrow, for which "misogyny" remains too insignificant and so rarely used a word, and for which murder is both an inadequate and repetitive description, even as this book goes to publication. The Shakespearean--Freudian slipknot: that women and women's bodies were like flowers, that flowers we would never know the herstory or names of, would cast a spell as sweet — intrigued and challenged, obsessed and kept awakening me in the dark.

Somewhere I had heard that the murders in Montreal that day had taken place within ten minutes. Women's bodies, like innocent, beautiful flowers, cut down. Whether this clocking measurement was true or not, the idea was an apocryphal indication of the transient brevity and rarity of human life, the unpredictability of fate.

That there was a woman who studied engineering, and was prevented from her reach for equality, independence, achievement, only by murder, and from ashes came the cri de coeur across the country, compelled me to return to this work. And hope. Never, never again. Never again will women in Canada be endangered, stalked, killed, not in their personal or professional lives. Declared in 1989. Yet this proactive, difficult, despair work to stop violence against women goes on, of necessity, to the present day.

The ephemeral elusiveness of life, so close and then at once so far away from one's own experience, smashed into the daily life experiences of many, the intelligences of us all, that this terrible event happened, actually happened, that this could happen to anyone, touched all of our lives. In any unexpected moment of time — this is what had changed forever, with December 6, 1989, in Montreal, Quebec, in Canada.

In the search for a way to express the intensity, sensitivity, light, colour, texture, scent of the experiences of women living full and strong and forthright lives, I was not alone. The creative impulse, the intent finally to not be writing just about this grief or this specific event, but with transcendence to artistic expression, peacemaking, remembering all the women loved, alive, taken too soon then and since. In women's artmaking employed historically, there are many instances of the essence of the physical and the spiritual reach combined. The extraordinary ordinary young women of L'École Polytechnique inspired me to try to capture the essence of flowers, their freedom of expression on Earth. In this winter garden, I found light, in each specific flowering wonder, and its naming, theme, style, shape, colour, provocation of feeling.

To be reminded that this work was necessary, more than artistic expression, I could not forget that I lived on the small island where the Canadian woman poet Pat Lowther, murdered by domestic violence, had spent family summers. The same beloved island where her bloody Vancouver marriage mattress had been found after her death. I had only to recall the melancholy of healing following that incident in what was now my own community years later, of a naked woman and her two tiny children who had been snatched from their beds, in pajamas, rescued off the beach in the same bay I lived in. They had spent the night in the cold, afraid to cry out, unable to see their way to look for help, wet and tired. I will never forget her bruised, exhausted face turning to the sunlight, her children's bodies draped like long-stemmed spent roses over her arms. She left our community to heal, to continue to address the ways and means to end violence against women, and children. Her heart-rending experiences, her protection of her children, and her courage to move on, sent my soul back to work. Look alive, her courage said to me. That is the only revenge. Be well. Do your best work.

The murders of fourteen women students changed our country, and changed feminism in Canada, following December 6, 1989, in Montreal. In many places, the efforts once again to stop violence against women were begun with new energy, even anger, certainly unshakable resolve. Each woman involved in this work had to find a way to continue to do this dark work, even in times of despair, this difficult work that the social, economic, political, religious, state and cultural constructs of Canada should already have accomplished. One can only do such work in the hope that success will come. With energy, without diminishment. A bouquet of flowers.

In the language of flowers, the history and study of that form, documenting, drawing, witnessing, communicating, the art and articulation of detail work, recording small changes, love's progress, in alternate and subversive forms, women have succeeded in many arts. An **abc**, a floral text, an illustrated notebook that tries to work out the unfathomable, to document the fact that a new sense of language is required, a new way of seeing, finding truth, working for peaceful co-existence and flourishing in life in terms of the lives and bodies of women is what's called for.

Against the unjustified, the inexcusable, the indefensible. Against the colonization of the hatred against women. Against violence, against fear, against murder. An incantation, a rant, an inspiration, chant, protest, rave, memento mori, invocation, prayer. Dense and demanding, a breviary with alphabet letters, woven with the meaning of flowers, the messages are many. Fourteen women died. Thirteen other women were wounded that same day. Nineteen names were on the list in the murderer's pocket. Despite healing messages and strengthened moral vision, the heart nevertheless breaks. One does not forget. "Because they were women…"

This long poem is small compared to the life of even one woman. To at least be a demonstration of love, a palm against death, a voice to prevent terrible loss, and move toward positive change is the hope. The stylized rant, more subtle incantations, the implicit, the explicit, the unmistakable woman's point of view, sensibility, strength, is the intent. To reclaim the flower, and flower language, in the long breath of women's work, artistic, linguistic, domestic, is the purpose. Love of other women, their unique voices and lives, is the celebration. To never give them up, but to keep remembering. To never give up being challenged by their loss, in moving forward in courage and women's accomplishments. In the work of many other women, in idea, art, concept, intellect, within nature, this work flowers in millions of colours. In art to change the world, to make a contribution, much to do.

I have been inspired by the dynamic, breathing, living language of flowers, an alphabet dance of what flowers mean, a translation from the sending of messages with flowers. With love, a bit extravagant, intense, with liberties. In revealing new work, heartfelt, the author wants at least to do no harm, with faith, to have no harm done. In the name of those for whom there is no justice, only remembrance, even re-opening memory and committing to publication takes courage. In the flowering of a new piece of writing, one is tempted to lay the medieval protection, or curse, as follows:

"If anyone take away this book, let him die the death…let the falling sickness and fever seize him, let him be broken on the wheel and hanged. Mea culpa. Amen."

Clearly, then, much more work to be done.

NOTES ON TEXT

Credits & influences & notes to the sympathetic reader:

epigraph (1): from *"The Illuminated Language of Flowers,"* Illustrated Kate Greenway, text Jean Marsh, Holt Rinehart, New York, 1978.

epigraph (2): from *"One Hundred Flowers,"* Georgia O'Keefe, Knopf, New York, 1989.

epigraph (3): from *In Search of Flowers of the Amazon Forests,* Margaret Mee, Nonesuch Expeditions, Suffolk, England, 1988.

epigraph (4): translated from the Swedish, blessing.

epigraph (5): from the poem, "Carapace," Cathy Ford, in *By Violent Means,* blewointment press, Vancouver and Toronto, 1983.

epigraph (6): from the poem, "Stillwater, Spillgate," Cathy Ford, in *the art of breathing underwater,* Mother Tongue Publishing, 2010.

epigraph (7): from the poem, "Letterknife, As Scissors, As Metaphor," Cathy Ford, in *By Violent Means,* blewointment press, Vancouver and Toronto, 1983.

Dedication: in memoriam, for the fourteen women who died, and the women who were injured in the Montreal Massacre, December 6, 1989, at L'École Polytechnique. Names of the fourteen women who were killed are entered alphabetically by last name through the opening thirteen sections of the long poem; with respect, only their first names are used within the body of the poem.

In memoriam:

Geneviève Bergeron - second year scholarship student, civil engineering, age 21.

Hélène Colgan - fourth year student in mechanical engineering, planning to take master's degree, age 23.

Nathalie Croteau - final year as mechanical engineering student, age 23.

Barbara Daigneault - fourth year student in mechanical engineering, worked as teaching assistant, age 22.

Anne-Marie Edward - first year student in chemical engineering, age 21.

Maud Haviernick - second year student in engineering materials, graduate in environmental design, age 29.

Barbara Klucznick Widajewicz - second year student specializing in engineering materials studies, age 31.

Maryse Laganière - employee in budget department of L'ecole Polytechnique, age 25.

Maryse Leclair - student in final year in mechanical engineering, age 23.

Anne-Marie Lemay - student in final year in mechanical engineering, age 27.

Sonia Pelletier - was to graduate December 7, 1989 in mechanical engineering; she was awarded her degree post-humously, age 28.

Michèle Richard - second year student in engineering materials, age 21.

Annie St-Arneault - second year mechanical engineering student, age 23.

Annie Turcotte - first year student in engineering materials, age 21.

(Names of the thirteen other women injured that day, and the names of the nineteen on a list in the murderer's pocket remain to be remembered.)

(author's note: under no circumstance has the name of the murderer of the women of Montreal killed on December 6, 1989 been allowed to enter into this text.)

Sources:

(a) *Globe and Mail*, Saturday, December 6, 1997: "Eight years later and the lump in my throat is still not gone," she said, "I still feel like I have been severed from my own blood and flesh." Suzanne Laplante-Edward, mother of Anne-Marie Edward, at the unveiling of Vancouver's Women's Monument Project in Thornton Park, December 6, 1997, designed by Beth Alper. Memorial's dedication promises to make a better world in memory of "all women who have been murdered by men". This message repeated in seven languages.
(b) "The War Against Women," report of the House of Commons Standing Committee on Health and Welfare, Social Affairs, Seniors and Status of Women.
(c) Canadian Advisory Council on the Status of Women.
(d) "A Handbook for the Prevention of Family Violence," developed by the Family Violence Prevention Project, of the Community Child Abuse Council of Hamilton-Wentworth, Ontario.
(e) Film, *After the Montreal Massacre*, Studio **d**, **cbc** Production.

Sections:

(1): "*to bring back the dead*" , in the name of hope, *Shaddai*, or reference by Maria Jacobs, in *Precautions Against Death*, to the translation given by I.B. Singer in *The Magician of Lublin*, "*the one who said enough*". Precautions Against Death, Maria Jacobs, Mosaic Press, Oakville, Ontario, 1983.

(2): "*after the garden gate, I enter in*", garden of Margaret Bennett, Mayne Island, B.C., and "*only memory wakes us*", reference to "*the murdered dreams awake*", Cathy Ford, Caitlin Press, Vancouver, B.C., 1979, 1980.

(3): inspiration, *Hana*, Yasuhiro Ishimoto, Chronicle Books, San Francisco, California, 1989, and less specifically, other photographers of flowers, and botanicals.

(4): inspiration, *In Search of Flowers of the Amazon Forest*, Margaret Mee, edited by Toni Morrison, Nonesuch Expeditions, Suffolk, England, 1988.

(5): inspiration, conversation with Tina Farmilo, artist, writer, child educator, Mayne Island, B.C. December 6, 1994, who said, "*…give me a language where one word means breath, means voice, means soul.*"

(6): with thanks, the poetry of Judith Fitzgerald, especially, *Ultimate Midnight*, Black Moss, 1992; *Rapturous Chronicles*, Mercury, 1991; *Diary of Desire*, Black Moss, 1987; and *Lacerating Heartwood*, Coach House, 1977.

(7): and thanks, the poetry and paintings of bill bissett, for faith, especially, *hard 2 beleev*, Talonbooks, 1990; and *th last photo uv th human soul, Talonbooks, 1993,* and countless more lifesavings.

(8): thanks too, the poetry of Carolyn Zonailo, especially *auto-da-fe*, blewointment press, 1977, and for the letters of the alphabet letters. And naturally the poetry of Phyllis Webb, especially and inclusive, *The Vision Tree - Selected Poems*, Talonbooks, 1982. Inspired by *"a question of questions"* and *"The Sea Is Also A Garden".*

(9): Finally and absolutely, those poets, painters, novelists and thinkers, who are my inspirational community of choice, in heart and mind: Mona Fertig, especially *4722 Rue Berri*, Caitlin Press, 1986; Maxine Gadd, Erin Mouré, Magie Dominic, Gay Allison, Mary di Michele, Anne Marriott, Dorothy Livesay, Anne Szumigalski, Sharon Nelson, Linda Rogers, Gwendolyn MacEwen, Phyllis Webb, Anne Burke, Dona Sturmanis, Roo Borson, Brenda Niskala, Lala Heine-Koehn, Jane Munro, Ingrid Klassen, Carolyn Zonailo, Ann Ireland, Audrey Thomas, Marilyn Bowering, Catherine Owen, Daphne Marlatt - all of whom challenge, provoke, inspire, but especially, examine women's lives in their work.

And Lorna Crozier, talking with Peter Gzowski, so long ago, on a wet winter day, CBC Radio, the snow falling sideways…sounds from the amazon…which sounded like: *"…somewhere where there are flowers we'll never know the name of…"* from which the title of this poem is drawn.

Also, revolutionaries in letters, written work, visual art, the female, feminist voice: Christine de Pizan in *The Book of the City of Ladies*, Frida Kahlo, Djuna Barnes, Gertrude Stein, Diane Wakoski in *Dancing on the grave of a son of a bitch*, Pat Lowther, Virginia Woolf, Violette le Duc, Judy Chicago, Colette, Toni Morrison, Anne Hébert, Marie Claire Blais, Elizabeth Smart, Nicole Brossard, Anne Waldman, Georgia O'Keefe, Emily Carr, Francine Prose, Gabrielle Roy, Francoise Sagan, Anne Sexton, Marina Warner, Jeannette Winterston, Isak Dinesen, many others.

(10): "pretty maids…" from the nursery rhyme, of course.

(11): inspired by: *"My Father"*, sung by Judy Collins, Rocky Mountain Park Music Co., Inc., on *Judy Collins*, Book of the Month Club Records, Camp Hill, Pennsylvania, U.S.A., 1981.

(12): *"O Holy Night"*, words and music by Adolphe Adams, sung by Rita Mc-Neill, *Now The Bells Ring*, Lupins Records, 1988, traditional Christmas carol.

(13): neither definitive, nor exhaustive, but including: *"The Montreal Massacre"* edited by Lousie Malette and Marie Chalouh, translated by Marlene Wildeman, gynergy books, Charlottetown, P.E.I., 1991; *she would be the first sentence of my next novel*, by Nicole Brossard, The Mercury Press, Toronto, Canada, 1998; *The Orchid*, P. Frances Hunt, photography T. Kijima, Spring Books, London, England, 1978; *Wild Flowers - Ferns and Grasses*, Bohumil Slavik, illustrated by Vlastimil Choc, Octopus Books, London, England, 1974; *Glorious Colour*, Kaffe Fassett, photography by Steve Lovi, Century, London, England, 1988; *Orchids, 1993 Calendar*, The Rod McLellan Acres of Co. Orchids, Landmark, Novato, California, 1993; *Fruits of the Earth - Flowers and Fruits in Needlepoint*, Hugh Ehrman, Simon and Schuster, New York, 1991; *The Illuminated Language of Flowers*, illustrated by Kate Greenaway, text by Jean Marsh, Holt, Rinehart and Winston, New York, 1978; *One Hundred Flowers*, Georgia O'Keefe, edited by Nicholas Callaway, Alfred A. Knopf, New York, 1989; *Twelve Months of Flowers*, John Bowles and Winterthus Museum Collection, Galison Book, New York, 1989; *Crows, an old rhyme*, pictures by Heidi Holder, Farrar, Straus Giroux, New York, 1987; *Birds, Beasts & Flowers*, selected by John Carroll, Webb & Bower, Exeter, England, 1981; *Through the Flower*, Judy Chicago, Doubleday, New York, 1975; *Beyond the Flower*, Judy Chicago, Viking / Penguin, New York, 1996; *The Dinner Party*, Judy Chicago, Viking / Penguin, New York, 1996; *The Concise Encyclopedia of Favorite Wild Flowers*, Marjorie J. Dietz, Doubleday & Company, Inc., Garden City, New York, 1965; *The Ladies' Flower Garden*, Wendy Hobson, Colour Library Books, Godallming, Surrey, England, 1993; *The Country Flowers of a Victorian Lady*, Fanny Robinson, based on *"A Book Of Memory"*, Apollo Publishing, Highgate, London, England, 1999; *The Wild Flowers of North America*, Creative Publishing, Bath, England, 1997 edition, Whitecap Books; from the original lithograph edition, Botanical Fine Arts Weekly, New York, New York, 1894; *The Birthday Book*, Jane Newdick, Neil Sutherland, and Jo Finnis, David Squire, and Robyn Bryant, editors, Tormont Publications, Montreal, Quebec, 1992; *A Regency Lady's Faery Bower*, Amelia Jane Murray, Holt, Rinehart and Winston, New York, 1985; *A Canadian Country Diary*, Ruth Mason, Hownslow Press, Willowdale, Ontario, 1982.

(14): alphabetizing of the text in section 14 is done on the flowers' name, or on the meaning of the flower's name, interwoven. Emphasis in the text on giving feminist voice to naming and meaning.

- d - reference: Billy Holiday, blues singer, American; Virginia Woolf, novelist, British.

- f - reference: *Red Canna, 1924,* painting by Georgia O'Keefe, painter, American.

- i - reference: *Red Canna, 1923,* painting by Georgia O'Keefe, as above, and *Petunia and Coleus, 1924,* same.

- j - reference: *Purple Petunia, No. 2, 1924,* painting by Georgia O'Keefe, as above.

- k - reference: *"I will always love you",* written and sung by Dolly Parton; *"Nothing compares to you",* written and sung by Sinead O'Connor. Both timeless.

- k- poinsettia nine to twelve foot hedges, St. Vincent, West Indies, December 1986.

- p - reference: works by Anaïs Nin, French novelist; works by Maria Jacobs, Canadian poet, editor, publisher; reference Aimeé Martin, French writer, letters to his wife Sophia on Natural History influenced many other writers and use of flower language.

- q - reference, *queen of everything,* Anna Parisella Thomas, Mayne Island, 1994.

- r - reference: on revenge, Audrey Thomas, in friendship, tenacity, and in continued inspiration for writing as well as one can, every time.

- s - reference: estimate nine million women killed as witches, probably more; medieval witch trials, ad infinitum.

- t- reference: hours spent in the garden of Sharon Nelson, Canadian poet and editor, Montreal, Quebec, May 1985, etc.

- v - reference: Jack-in-the-Pulpit, No. 1, No. 2., No. 3., No. 4., No. 5., paintings by Georgia O'Keefe, all 1930.

- x- *"the opened eye"*, from *"dear emily, I've seen your trees"*, in *the murdered dreams awake*, by Cathy Ford, Caitlin Press, Vancouver, B.C., 1979, 1980.

- y - reference: Abstraction No. 3 - 1927, or (Ballet Skirt, or Electric Light, 1927), painting by Georgia O'Keefe. And reference, remembrance, ceremony for the Montreal 14, December 6, 1994, Mayne Island, B.C.

- first draft of section 14 of "Flowers we will never know the names of" was first performed at "Live at the Ag", a Mayne Island Little Theatre performance evening, December 2 and 3, 1994, Mayne Island, B.C.; credits in text drawn from original introduction of 5th anniversary commemoration of Montreal Massacre. On December 6, 1994, fourteen women representing women against violence against women (WAVAW)and one baby boy, nascent, marked the anniversary date by floating red carnations, white snowdrops, golden wheat stalks, lit candles, in paper boats, on the ocean off Oyster Bay, below Maude Bay, down from Georgina Point Lighthouse, Mayne Island, B.C. Remembrances continue across Canada.

Special thanks to Mona Fertig, visionary, courageous publisher of Mother Tongue; Mark Hand for his beautiful and sensitive book design; Janet Dwyer for her fine photograph for the cover; and Jo-Ann Way for her care with my author photograph.